BREATHE AND BE

For my brother Bob
KATE COOMBS

For my godchildren,
Oiva and Auni
ANNA EMILIA LAITINEN

The trees are the lungs of this planet Earth.
Let's take care of them, so they breathe for us.

Sounds True
Boulder, CO 80306

Text © 2017 by Kate Coombs
Illustrations © 2017 by Anna Emilia Laitinen

Sounds True is a trademark of Sounds True, Inc.
All rights reserved. No part of this book may be
used or reproduced in any manner without written
permission from the author, illustrator, and publisher.

Published 2017

Cover design by Rachael Murray
Book design by Beth Skelley

Printed in South Korea

Library of Congress Cataloging-in-Publication Data
Names: Coombs, Kate, author. | Laitinen, Anna Emilia, illustrator.
Title: Breathe and be : a book of mindfulness poems / by Kate Coombs ;
illustrations by Anna Emilia Laitinen.
Description: Boulder, CO : Sounds True, Inc., 2017.
Identifiers: LCCN 2017002584 (print) | LCCN 2017023792 (ebook) |
  ISBN 9781622039388 (ebook) | ISBN 9781622039371 (hardcover)
Subjects: LCSH: Mindfulness (Psychology—Juvenile poetry. |
  Buddhism—Juvenile poetry.
Classification: LCC PS3603.O5796 (ebook) |
  LCC PS3603.O5796 A6 2017b (print) | DDC 811/.6—dc23
LC record available at https://lccn.loc.gov/2017002584

10 9 8 7 6 5 4 3 2 1

BREATHE AND BE

A Book of Mindfulness Poems

Kate Coombs

illustrated by

Anna Emilia Laitinen

sounds true
BOULDER, COLORADO

I breathe slowly in,
I breathe slowly out. My breath
is a river of peace.
I am here in the world.
Each moment I can breathe and be.

What am I thinking?
What comes and goes in my mind?
I watch my thoughts.
They swim by like little fish.
They shine blue, green, red, yellow.

There's a quiet place
in my head like an egg hidden
in a nest. A place
I go when the world is loud.
A moss-green forest with birds.

I see the world new—
my friends with bright sneakers,
the fresh smell of grass,
a line of ants winding by.
I see each for the first time.

Sometimes I'm a cloud.
Sometimes a mountain or a stone.
Sometimes I'm a river,
a small seed or a great tree.
But I am always me.

When days crash thunder
and throw lightning around
I am still, watching.
I am a calm umbrella
inside the blue and gray storm.

How I rush rush rush!
Thoughts flutter and dart like birds.
Slow down, thoughts.
Come quictly with me.
There is time to breathe and be.

Some days I bark and snap
like a little dog. Instead
I will be a tree.
Leaves, branches, roots—patient
in summer, in fall, winter, spring.

I watch the stream.
Each thought is a floating leaf.
One leaf is worry,
another leaf is sadness.
The leaves drift softly away.

I see myself
by the ocean, toes touching sand,
fingers finding a shell
at the edge of blue water.
Where is your quiet place?

Tomorrow's an egg
that hasn't hatched. Yesterday
is a bird that has flown.
But today is real. Here now,
this minute, the true wings.

The caterpillar
and the tadpole are becoming
something more
and I am becoming more me,
my heart filling up with it.

My feet touch earth.

My hands touch tall grasses.

My face touches sky.

I run through the morning.

I am alive in this world!

I breathe slowly in,
I breathe slowly out. My breath
is a pathway of peace
moving softly through me.
Each day I can breathe and be.

Mindfulness is an idea that comes from Buddhism, a religion based on the teachings of Gautama Buddha, who was born in India around 500 BC. Buddhism is practiced throughout Asia and has also given rise to many meditation practices in the Western world. The poems about mindfulness in this book are written using a Japanese poetry form called *tanka*, an earlier version of the well-known haiku. A tanka has five lines, which in English are often divided into syllables of 5, 7, 5, 7, 7. However, poets sometimes write them more broadly in a pattern of five lines that are short, long, short, long, long.

To learn more about mindfulness, start by looking for the works and words of Jon Kabat-Zinn (creator of Mindfulness-Based Stress Reduction) and Thich Nhat Hanh (Buddhist monk and peace activist). Kabat-Zinn has defined mindfulness as "the awareness that arises through paying attention on purpose, in the present moment, and non-judgmentally." He has also said, "It's about living your life as if it really mattered, moment by moment by moment by moment." Or as Thich Nhat Hanh explains, mindfulness is "the miracle which can call back in a flash our dispersed mind and restore it to wholeness so that we can live each minute of life."